Ode to a Commode

CONCRETE POEMS

Brian P. Cleary

iLLUSTRATiONS BY
Andy Rowland

M MILLBROOK PRESS/MINNEAPOLIS

For Maryann,
Imani & Fatma
—BPC

For my little
pancake, Alice
—AR

Millbrook Press
A division of Lerner Publishing Group, Inc.
241 First Avenue North
Minneapolis, MN 55401 USA

For reading levels and more information, look up this title at www.lernerbooks.com.

Main body text hand-lettered by Andy Rowland.

Library of Congress Cataloging-in-Publication Data

Cleary, Brian P., 1959–
    [Poems. Selections]
    Ode to a commode: concrete poems/ By Brian P. Cleary ; Illustrated by Andy Rowland.
        pages   cm. — (Poetry Adventures)
    ISBN: 978-1-4677-2045-8 (lib. bdg. : alk. paper)
    ISBN: 978-1-4677-4767-7 (eBook)
    I. Rowland, Andrew, 1962- ill. II. Title.
    PS3553.L39144C66 2014
    811'.54—dc23   2013030859

Manufactured in the United States of America
1 – DP – 7/15/14

TABLE OF CONTENTS

What Is a Concrete Poem?

When you think of poems, you probably think of words in straight lines. But some poems actually look like animals or objects! The verses can be curvy, jagged, or even round. These kinds of poems are called concrete poems.

A concrete poem takes on the shape of whatever it is about. The topic of the poem is always an object (instead of a feeling or an idea). The letters, words, or symbols are arranged on the page to form a picture of that object. So a poem about a flight of stairs is actually shaped like a flight of stairs. In this fun, visual type of poetry, the words and their shape work together to create the poem.

Look at the poem on the right-hand page. Even if you just glance at it from several feet away and can't make out the words, you can tell that it's a pair of scissors. Now read the piece:

Scissors snip and nip and cut and always come in pairs.
Great for cutting paper up and trimming my sister's dolls' hairs.

Making concrete poems is easier than you might think. Pick something that has an interesting shape. Write a poem about it, and then shape the lines of the poem to look like what you chose. You can make the shape by hand, or you can use a computer.

Not a big rhymer? Not a problem. Concrete poems don't have to rhyme. Just write descriptive words and phrases. It will still look really cool.

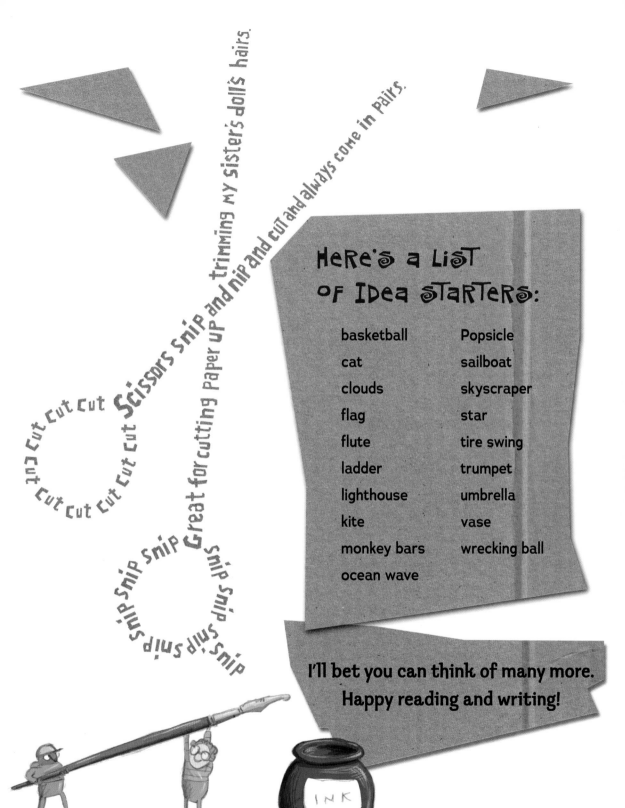

Scissors snip and nip and cut and always come in pairs.

Cut Cut Cut Cut Scissors snip and nip and trimming my sister's doll's hairs.

Cut Cut Cut Cut Cut Cut Cut Cut Cut

Snip Snip Snip Snip Great for cutting paper up and

Snip Snip Snip Snip Snip Snip

HeRe's a LisT oF IDea STaRTeRs:

basketball   Popsicle

cat   sailboat

clouds   skyscraper

flag   star

flute   tire swing

ladder   trumpet

lighthouse   umbrella

kite   vase

monkey bars   wrecking ball

ocean wave

I'll bet you can think of many more.
Happy reading and writing!

INK

ODE TO A COMMODE

Flush goes the sound of the toilet! The water (with everything in it) vanishes in a swirl and a whoosh, and the bowl fills back up in a minute!

NO WONDER HE'S SO QUIET

LEAF ON THE TREE, EACH BLADE OF GRASS, BLUE JAY, OR ANT, I ALSO FOUND OUT NOW I CAN WHAT I THOUGHT WAS REALLY POTTED SEE EVERY WAS MY FRIEND A TALL PLANT.

THE LAST PIECE OF HALLOWEEN CANDY

Once I lived inside a store atop a candy shelf.
Now I'm stuck alone inside this bag all by myself.

Hard and shiny colored candies, soft and chewy gummies
all once were my neighbors here — a whole block's worth of yummies.

The candy that's most popular was long ago selected,
opened, and then gobbled up, while I remain neglected.

The caramel treats have been enjoyed, the nutty chocolate savored,
but no one wants a candy bar that's "Tuna Salad" flavored.

FANS will clap for kickers as I'M SAILING THROUGH The POST. AND WHEN I'm caught, receivers get to be THE ONES who boast. AND when I'm CARRIED past the goal, just look around and see—the cheers are for the RUNNING back, but why AREN'T they FOR ME?

WHAT ABOUT ME?

A TWISTED TALE

Sometimes you're soft and you're chewy and warm and sometimes you're crunch. And sometimes you're hard and you have an unusual, interesting form, and you're always delicious with lunch.

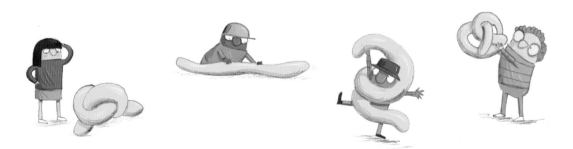

AiR SHOW

Diving, sweeping, cursive loops, rounder, wider, opening up loops, speeding toward the window glass... this is one exciting class!....

TICK, TICK, TOCK, TICK, TICK, TOCK.

SCHOOL BELL RINGS AT 3 O'CLOCK. YAY!

TIME-OUT

Orange or blue and full of helium floating up to reach the ceili-um

string string string string string string

GOING UP

A LiTTLe HaiRY

Our new crossing guard has the grandest mustache.
It's thick and it's brown and it's fancy.
Not everyone could make whiskers look good,
but they sure look terrific on Nancy!

STOP A BIT, BRITT.
WHOA, JOE. TAKE A BREAK,
JAKE. DO NOT PROCEED, RASHEED.
HOLD ON, JUAN. CEASE, DENISE.
USE THE BRAKES ON YOUR BIKE, MIKE.
STAY WHERE YOU ARE, SUNDAR,
YOU NEED TO WAIT, KATE. SUSPEND YOUR ACTION,
JACKSON. HOLD OFF ON THE PEDAL, GRETEL. YOU'VE
GOT ALL DAY, AKSHAY. STOPPING'S THE PLAN, ANNE.
DON'T KEEP ON GOIN', OWEN. TAKE A SECOND AND
CHILL, BILL. DON'T MAKE THAT LEAP,
SANDEEP. HOLD STEADY, EDDY. D O N O T
ADVANCE, LANCE. STOP IN YOUR TRACKS,
MAX. DON'T GO ON. D'SHAWN.
HAVE A SEAT, PETE. CATCH YOUR BREATH, BETH.
HALT, I SAY, JAY. STAY IN YOUR
PLACE, GRACE. DON'T GO, ALEJANDRO.
KICK BACK AWHILE, KYLE.

STOP

15

HI-HO, SILVERWARE!

WHETHER IT'S TWISTING SPAGHETTI

OR STABBING SOME VEGGIES OR PORK, WHEN THE TIME COMES TO EAT, IT'S NOT EASY TO BEAT THE SIMPLE AND PRACTICAL FORK.

BRRRR

THE COAL FOR MY EYES, I LIKE VERY MUCH. THE BRIGHT ORANGEY CARROT'S A COLORFUL TOUCH. BUT THE BUNDLED-UP KIDS WHO CREATED ME CHOSE JUST A SCARF AND A HAT AS MY ONLY WARM CLOTHES!

AN INVITATION

A STAR THAT SHIMMERS AS YOUR CROWN AND NECKLACES OF LIGHT. SHINY JEWELS OF BLUE AND RED AND SILVER, GOLD, AND WHITE. TINSELED ARMS OUTSTRETCHED AS IF TO WELCOME US AND SAY, "COME IN—ENJOY THE WONDER OF THIS MAGIC HOLIDAY."

BEST FISHES

MACKEREL AND TUNA, PERCH AND BASS AND SCROD. SAILFISH AND GROUPERS, IN THE WATER THOUSAND TYPES OF FISHES. SOME ARE SMALL AND

HERRING, MARLIN, COD, SNAPPERS, TROUT AND THERE ARE SEVERAL AND BIG AND SOME ARE MANY ARE DELICIOUS.

THE PLAN

Whatever you reach for, when you aim to do it, "one step at a time" is the surest way to it. Focus and practice and learn and rehearse. The step that is hardest to take is the first.

THE BOA CONSTRICTOR

my diet is unusual, so based on how I feel, I might just have a lizard or a lizard or a monkey, and now and then a pig and wild pigs and rats on several mice to munch. I'd tell you more, but I've got my favorite snacks a couple birds for lunch. hiss hiss hiss hiss

I Chews You

You're juicy, sweet, and flavorful. You're stretchy, wet, and yummy. It's weird that you're delicious, yet never reach my tummy. If I should puff and puff enough, you're airy, round, and fat. Just like a tiny pink balloon that ends up going SPLAT!

ALL WET

Sprinkler

Wet and clean and crisp and cold.

energizing, brisk, and bold.

Running, splashing, sliding bliss.

I wonder — just whose lawn is this?.

MY BROTHER'S SHOE

It isn't some milk
that's been spilled in
the car. It isn't a three-
day-old diaper or an
overripe basket of
cheeses or fruits that every
few minutes smells riper.
This isn't the egg that was hidden for Easter
and found when Thanksgiving was through.
No—this is the smell that can only be found
wafting out of my big brother's shoe.

I'LL HAVE A
SCOOP OF ALMOND
FUDGE AND ONE
OF BRAMBLE BERRY,
A SCOOP OF ROCKY ROAD
AND ONE OF TRIPLE
CHOCOLATE—CHERRY.
I'LL HAVE ONE MORE OF
BUBBLE GUM AND
TWO OF CARAMEL CRUNCH
AND ALSO PEANUT BUTTER SWIRL
(IT'S KIND OF CLOSE
TO LUNCH). LET'S ADD A
SCOOP OF APRICOT AND
TWO OF LEMON CUSTARD
AND ONE PAPAYA
PUMPKIN, PLEASE, AND
ONE OF MANGO MUSTARD.
I'LL HAVE TWO SCOOPS OF
PEACH AND ONE OF
PEPPERMINTY
PRUNE. I'D
ADD ONE OF
VANILLA,
...BUT...
I DON'T
HAVE
ANY
ROOM
!

COOL, SWEET...
BUT ENOUGH
ABOUT ME

Red, White, and You

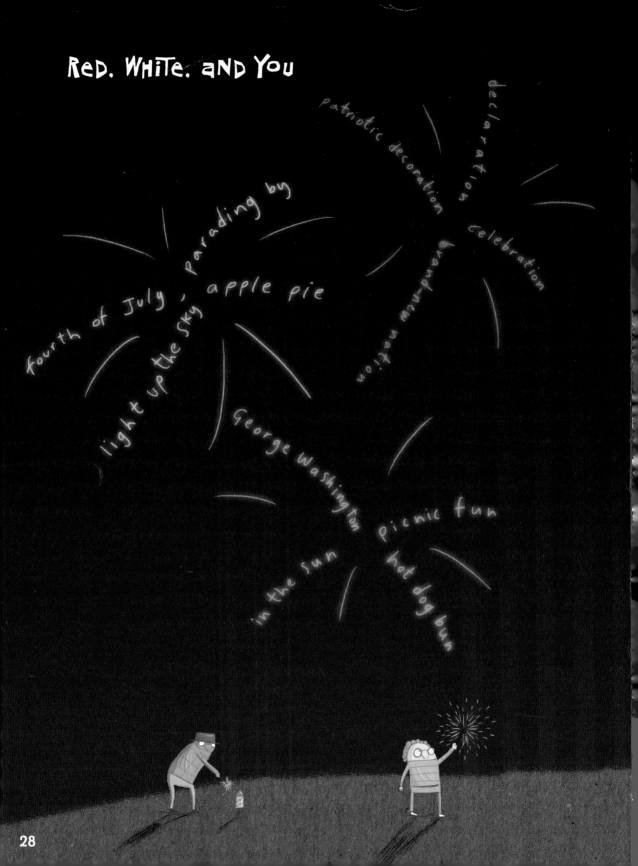

fourth of July
parading by
apple pie
light up the sky
patriotic decoration
declaration
celebration
grandfather nation
George Washington
picnic fun
in the sun
hot dog bun